For You to Heal

Poetry in the tending and mending

by

Joe Bisicchia

Cyberwit.net
HIG 45 Kaushambi Kunj, Kalindipuram
Allahabad - 211011 (U.P.) India
http://www.cyberwit.net
Tel: +(91) 9415091004 +(91) (532) 2552257
E-mail: info@cyberwit.net

ISBN: 978-93-95224-11-6

First Edition: 2022
Rs. 200/-

Printed in India at VCORRE LLP.

Acknowledgements

For You to Heal

"Patient"	– published by The Poet's Haven, 2016
"Ho'oponpono"	– published by Tipton Poetry Journal, 2016
"Hope is More Than a Placebo"	– published by The Poet's Haven, 2016
"My Chest X-ray"	– published by The Poet's Haven, 2016
"Beyond This Cancer"	– published by The Poet's Haven, 2016
"Poor Historian"	– published by Sentinel Literary Quarterly, 2018
"Nursing Home Piano"	– published by Paragon Press, Anapest, 2018
"Day 49 in a Burn Unit"	– published by Quail Bell Magazine, 2018
"Nurse's Rounds"	– published by Chronogram Magazine, 2020
"Waiting on a Miracle"	– published by A&U, America's AIDS Magazine, 2020

Contents

For You

I feel a poem coming on.
To be followed by another, and another.
Sign of life, that's what it is.
Sign of forever, too.

I drift, but not alone. You are here.
Via everyone. It's a shared space.
Self by self by self, by all of us
as one.

We each long to be healed.
So near the healer, if only we knew.
So near to heal each other.
So near to let go and be healed.

What shall follow is a moment in time
now over and over, for countless selves.
Old and new.
I feel a poem coming on.

To be followed by another, and another.
Each to groove near the heart,
much better than squeezed cigarettes.
Got a pack of poems in my chest pocket.

For You.

Caretakers

You are my father
in your voice.

You are my mother
in your eyes.

You are my sister
in your smile.

You are my brother
in your trust.

You are my friend,
just as You are.

You are my joy,
and I am Yours.

Knocked to the Ground

And you speak to me.

How far, the long road ahead?
The venom in me
reviles this bad break,
its distaste,
and how it discolors all of me.

Such heavy need to believe
the scales will fall from my eyes
and true colors will again be seen.

Throw away this vast ego of mine
and let me again fly like you do,
with belief..

There is that never-ending beep.
And, above it, your hopeful clatter.
And you speak to me of healing.

I can hear you as just a single fly,
the one buzzing now at the glass
so near my very soul and sill.
I can sense all the universe you see
not only in the energy of your wings,
but in your vision of hope
as if you won't ever stop believing.
In my healing.

My Bad Break

Maybe it loomed,
or not, came and went
but stayed.
Maybe it is
with me now, but
owns me not.

Some may say
I'm shaped by it,
defined by it.

I say, I shall rise
to this occasion of now.
Maybe every moment
I loom.
And so, I shall be.
Not broken, but one.
Blessed.

You are here.

And I'm not alone.

In Line for a Heart

There is a scar where my heart used to be.
The sad part is not the scar but this—
the seemingly missing heart.
Sad for me and others.
I worry how many of us there are.

Maybe soon night will be advanced,
and day at hand in neighborhoods distant,
in neighborhoods nearby enough.

And steam shall lift from the lids, faraway
the line of green trash cans,
each as if now is now to be lived, each filled
with weeklong lost, each soon shallow again,
each soon emptied for landfill.

But the lost and tossed heart?

Sad for me and others. Yes,
I worry how many of us there are.

Armor Softens

Reality is unwound.
All of us are equal
under a hospital gown.

Patient

Window would see
world
if eyes weren't stuck
          bedside.

I'm stopped incapacitated,
yet
the aforementioned world
runs.

When I was young
I would show my face.
I used to dress myself
and go where I wanted.

But now,
with dull wall
and nurse down the hall,
I stretch out my hand
                    and wait.

Clock Melts

Goes at an altered speed now.
Now goes.
Maybe stands still, or not.
Hard to tell.
But, can't tell time what to do.

You lose your hair,
but like leaves in spring.
We hate the waiting, but even more
hate the hurrying.

All the while, you might think
of making pets of the random flies.
They nudge up against the glass
and want to get outside,
just like you.

But I am here.

The universe cannot lie.
It is here, bedside.
You would welcome a visitor
to pull the splinter, wide as a thorn,
big as the sky.

And so, you and I,

we walk the seashore corridor
in our matching hearts.
And time moves at the glass.
No matter the dull to the floor,
we see each other shine
as we are, walking on water.

Letting in the Light in Room 314

Her twin little brother
often stands in the threshold with a smile.
Has this kite he likes to hold. Ever polite,
allows in the unsuspecting docs and nurses.
Stands there patiently for a while.

All will be okay. Time to time, he leaves
and she sees a kite in sky in the nearby pane.
Last time she saw him alive he too was here,
in a hospital garment unflattering. Eyes
closed, and his mind supposedly was closed.
She spoke to him. And to the nurse's surprise,
and hers, his lips trembled as if he knew.

Then he soon wore new shoes. And new suit,
as the world rolled him past stained glass walls.

And now, her brother stands by with a smile.
All will be okay. And why? Her brother knows.
He knows everything there is to know.
Knows she loves him. Always did.
Even without the words. And after this,
there will be a kite in the sky. His.

War Buddy

Together, we survived Tet,
he says, even though
I know I wasn't even born yet.
But all's fair in jungles
and war and my father knows best.

His muscle is gone,
but his eyes are like skies
and I think I see something
of forever inside and he sees
something of forever in me.

He says I saved him once,
but he saved me twice. And
I sometimes think maybe, yes,
I was in mind back then
and saved him even though
I wasn't born yet, back when
he saved me twice somewhere
in the jungles of Tet.

Sometimes he cries
when he sees me because
he thought he had last seen me
dead, thought he had left me,
all of me, all my pieces back there,
back there in the jungle, and then
he cries. He cries when he realizes,
yes, we survived Tet.

Presence in Memorial's Garden

I sometimes talk to my mother about it.
About my father.
How he lost his face in the war.
I have asked what a face is for.

My father is sometimes hard to recognize
but he seems always so pleased to meet me
here or wherever this here is we are.
Firm is his hand shake, and his windows
go wide as if curious and readily able
to seek without fear of being seen.

Just this morning, we spiritedly laughed,
he and I, at the moment on the patio outside
a butterfly crossed our path, and dawdled
playfully about his hollow face, then to sky.
Me, thinking it was my mother,
knowing her grace never too far away.
He maybe did as well, filling the hollow
as he lingered a smile.

He says she says that is what a face is for.

Visiting Where the Leper Lives

Welcome
under my tiny, peeling roof,
this untidy, obscure, abandoned abode.
Kick off your shoes and feel at home.

By some miracle,
so much to share
being you've reached out, touched
and cared with the sun now upon the sill.

Feel free to leave when you want.
But free to stay here still. If you want.
Find love enough to heal. By God, find love.
Your presence is love.

And I see God in you.

Who do you somehow see?

Hospital Census

Am I this patient?
Am I that patient?
Am I all of these, face to face?
Am I able to hear all the angels
in a stethoscope?

Heartbeat by heartbeat.

So much hurting.
So much in need of healing.
So much of heaven in every heart.
So much going on in this place.
Room by room.

Windows of Our Wing

Each pane,
an eye to paradise.
From within,
and from the outside.

Here's a story, and
over here is another.

We know not the siloes.
But, all together,
a forever.
A moment, awake.
Or not.

So go we.

My current roommate,
she shuts her eyes.
TV never sleeps.
And to her right,
with love of life
she chases the mountains
never too far to reach.

And wraps her arms
around them.

And then
sets them free

to chase after her.
And me.

Spirit of St. Louis

Yes, it has been a long flight
but my propellers dutifully still sing
like ventilators tied to my being.

And, to my long flying eyes,
here in this medical university,
on a hospital bed in Missouri,
I look up at squared ceiling tiles.

Surely, amidst the city blocks of Paris,
there it is, the Eifel Tower.
And I'm looking down upon it.

O, I know that someone erudite,
a doctor or nurse, would disagree,
saying it's drug induced and only
a ceiling's little fire sprinkler dangling.

And what would I know?
I'm no pilot, but just an old barber.
I've never been to Paris, nor over it.
Certainly, never walked its streets,
never turned its corners, never
dropped shadows like Lindbergh did.

Until now.

Flat on my back, with nothing to do
but look up.

Bridge Outside 303B

By day,
through the hospital window
above the nearby river,
it is a river in its own way.
And it carries the sun
bumper-to-bumper.

At night,
each headlight combines
for streaming flight,
grateful for survival
held up high on this rainbow.

Car after car after car
after car despite
the pain, the slow uphill burn,
the height, and slow downhill slide.

He senses the glide of shooting stars.
And realizes so goes life,
with all its exhaust, simply a ride.

He sees himself in this mirror.
And all the people ever known,
or unknown.

He knows so, so many slip on by,
seemingly in the blur, but
he senses deep in his heart,
not one is alone.

For each is heading home.

Visiting Hour, Room 216

This one looks across the difficult distance
and wonders of the air.

It's been a while since she's visited here.

Is it mixture of mothballs and mother?
Or is it just the closeness of this room?

Some kind of bug
darts across the clock face.

Meanwhile, from across the bedside table,
the patient's hand outstretches to her
a plate of uneaten string beans.

And a smile finally

as the mother remembers and understands.

Neither had ever liked string beans.

It is then,
joyful eyes recognize
and remind the two of them of who they are.

They are as they are.

Home.

Cast in Suite 6

His father's foot fits snugly into the boot of Italy.
As for here, in this recovery room, same.

Immigrant plasterer had slipped on bottom rung.
A broken bone now tended to by the physician.

The patient is the father, and the physician the son.
And the old man is sometimes slow to complain.

Marvels instead at how the dust has cleared,
and how his son went on to become a foot doctor.

That, and well, maybe yet another reminder.
Would this kid finally find time to comb that hair?

Art in 332

So much to see and do
as I drift off to the fringe unglued.

Aside my bed, away from the flickering
box of cable news, red roofed homes arise
in a frame betwixt properly placed evergreens,
perfect paint just the same, all to genuinely
welcome me supposedly here
in flower bed's foreground, here again
to this brushed canvas,
as if I just came across this to find myself
wandering to where I am bruised, wondering
how far I have come and will have to go.

I sense I won't truly breathe the depicted knoll,
nor ever grow to know all the brushed flowers
more than this rushed and cold commode.

But, for this moment, I feel some kind of
lingering peace
as if a bird softly nesting
to one day soon fly, but now unseen
in one of the distant, almost overlooked
evergreens.

West Tower Sundowners

O, for souls to bend our petals anew
upon the hill, over the pain,
and to plant our hope like seeds.
Like mornings lifted by the sun.

And then we shall again arise.
But far too soon slip afar,
as the fading sun easily runs to hide
ever more a sadness, the emptying
of the hourglass.

Without any understanding,
we may follow clock's swords
as they swipe all the field of its colors.
And wonder of the loss of ourselves.
The loss of peace.

Peace is a field of daylilies.
Hope is patient in the obscurity,
but wilts to earth, and is mourned
even as we sleep,
which is far too often never too deep.

Seems,
no more peace, no more sleep, or
far too much.

O, for souls to bend our petals anew.
O, for souls to hold onto our hands,
so to save a fragile bud.

Busy Legs in 202

So much seems still. So much blurred.
There it goes, worse than any varicose,
I suppose a sense of my many roads,
the fear of a dead end. Or the runs instead.
Yet, to the apropos commodes, we go.
We run.

I do, and never alone, even though
I have long gone flat in this museum,
this room adorned by classics on the wall
like this one by Caspar David Friedrich,
The Monk by the Sea.
Maybe it is not here, but in my dreams.

Or a hospital window, just the same.
Maybe a view of God, or God knows what,
underneath.

Last night I walked with Jesus upon the sea.
He does my PT.
And He and I tonight shall proceed.
Yes, hand in hand we do, with ease
across the shine of this hospital floor.

Drum Major in 411

For the janitor in the haze, it is just a quick mop of the hospital floor here, but maybe the best part of the parade of floats, flying batons, tubas, horses, and clowns. Each performer endures the walking way, balancing the crossbeam. And in the steady wind, the beeping beats, and all the static in between, the procession provides each of us enough room for horns and banging drums. No wonder we lose our ears.

We might adjust the world to better hear so to see, but the runaway sun is faraway somewhere, a tiny yellow balloon with a slippery string too greasy to hold on to. And yet only a stethoscope away.

A rat-a-tat-tat is heard, just another precious heartbeat.

Sure as this janitor's present lead in rhythm, this wand, this spirited hum, this enthusiasm. It's amidst all the heartbeat, above all the buzz and beeps and it feels so right as the floor now has a healing sheen so that all might share the gleam in the eyes. So, yes, hear it. It says all of us have a shared rhythm in an opus of ourselves capped by a somewhere smile despite all the pain, streaming this parade of who we all once were, shall be, as we are.

Pulse

Our greatest dance is simplicity
with serendipity, every moment
by moment, from the heart,
more than by chance,
but by allowance as if given
by an all knowing discipline.

This nature of ours is as it is
from its start, a miracle.

So steady all weary hands
and steady all trembling knees
and straighten all paths, all veins.

And, as weakened as we once seemed,
now see us as we are, of invincible beep.
The aforementioned beep.
And the beep again.
And the beeps ahead to mention yet again.
Sound of life, maybe, indeed.
The persistent reminder of the seed
for each deep within a heartbeat.

We all want peace,
but not a silencing for it to be.
Know what shall never end.

So it is, take my hand and my being,
the injured limb will not be maimed,
and we shall walk, shall run,
shall dance again.

Dance on 5 North

Yes, it has a contagious way about it.
Yes, maybe it's even viral despite all our virus.
Yes, let us be as we simply are, minus the stuff
we are not, all that crud we are needing to shake.

Yes, in rhythm and rhythm, life rumbles inside
as a gift in rhythm and rhythm, that which is
consistent, honest, that which should never hide,
despite its depth far within the chest.

Put aside the disco ball glitter, but find heart.
Hospital delirium is true. It rolls in like a fog.
And may never leave here, but it must.
All along, there is a heartbeat to tend to.

We are so gifted with ability and connectivity,
that which endures as true. That which is
magical, ever complex and simple for it to beat,
our greatest dance despite any disability.

Whatever our hardship may now prove to be,
let us be this, us, by gift, by gift, by simply grace
so that we no longer even notice that which hurts,
that which has been holding us back. Let us give.

There should be no difference between the one
tending, and the one mending. Same dance.
No need to be a wallflower, but one bouquet.
Even if we still have to stay tight to our bed.

Make it a flower bed. Let's move our petals. And all our colors. And in the ongoing rhythm and rhythm, as we are, extraordinarily, let us simply dance to our shared heartbeats.

So it is to be lives lived.

Harden Not Your Heart

Despite her cloak, she speaks
as the wind exhales over my chest.
Despite our distance, she speaks.
Distance is lined with mountains
with faraway granite. But nearby
hills bend and break, undulate these
hospital sheets. She says to believe.
Faith shall do what it does.
Piles the mountains into my heart.

Seems I am moved with alacrity,
gurney to gurney, I guess. Perhaps
I shall follow the staff of Hermes,
or is it that of Asclepius? Perhaps
I have long lost myself
in some healing of Greek mythology.

Perhaps this is not stuff of allegory.

No, indeed, I follow reality
of the aforementioned voice.
I have no choice. But, am blessed.
I know where I now finally am.
Face to face to hard mountains.
Impossible to scale.
All of me may soon coarsen to stone.

I am not alone. And that is the blessing.

My Angel

She leads me. And I welcome it.

Rather than thicken me,
all my veins, I break apart to remake.

Rather than harden, I long to hearten
my heart instead.

Tell me your name, I think I say,
as the tunnel opens for me to breathe.

So much of me is surely sickening.
And yet, by her accompanying me,
I surely am and remain ever lovely.

I do know this angel's name already.
There is bloom in her kind eyes.

The hospital bedsheet tightens but
the soil under me softens enough
for daisies.

Surgery Prep

Silent my speech, out my teeth,
my dentures, ear piece.

Compress all noise to wring
as if the nearby waves,
now faraway drifting.

I'm told everything will happen
with great speed.

Soon, I will be fast asleep.

All along my heart beats.

I let go.

Cure

Open.

Take me apart.

Now that you see
all that is in disarray,
find me.
Rearrange.

Know me.
As I am
beyond the diagnosis.

Know me.
As I am
and as I shall be.

For good.

Vespers in the OR

Cheers to pristine lightbulbs
somewhere atop this sterile room where
I have lost my insides. I shall rise
to the light, with measures of me
somewhere wheeled away. How sad
if the gift given to live comes with a

forgetfulness of whence it came.

I now remember.

Long ago in the past,
we all danced around the light.

Then,
the spry angels moved about and away,
so far away as if forever distant. Yet,
here they now are as if never gone,
still at every finger, at every breath.

And I am an angel, simply one of them.
I am the Lord's. O, to be so present,
even if so handicapped by the knife
of daily life.

And this daily life is where we live.

And see, the Lord is mine and yours.
Share a water ice with me. Cherry.

Share all the universe with me.
All the forever that is, sharing this
prayer with all the other angels here,
dancing around the light, the Lord's.
And we shall roll, roll and roll
the breezy corridors.

Corridors

Door by door by floors no one should be alone.
we shall float up and down these endless floors

and remind the sleepless of our sleeping flowers
so soon to awaken, now resting to the harmony

of the constellations, the buzz, the beeps of birds
room to room, the sun a wand dispersing beams

of ourselves. Everyone is worthy of home.
Especially those who feel so very homeless.

So, let us all ring the bells, cling the utensils and
widen the sunflower, for it is time for breakfast.

ICU

Your eyes.
I know now what stays as kind.
Despite all my darkness.
There is all your light.
Here now with me.

What matters is healed.
My body, meanwhile,
my mind,
so much seemingly so vital,
can drift away.

But the flowers remain.
The ones brought by your eyes.
All the colors from within.
All that is alive, all that is love.

God is Love.

I see God in your eyes.

I sense you see God in mine.

Day 49 in the Burn Unit

red numbers in embers in timbers
after the inferno
arise next to my bed

seems they never fully extinguish
always grabbing at the fabric
at the fabric of my head

but she moves as if she owns them
sky queen
spreading before me her floating blue

her eyes are heaven
she smiles
and even the flames obediently listen

she lets go another snowflake pill
i swell under a water tower
needled by hose to within me

i dream
this place is in the distance
yet here

as the trees simmer
i wonder how they looked in spring
before the flames

of myself
i wonder the same thing
through the eyes of the sky queen

Nurse's Rounds

…patient
love is
kind love
is patient
love is
kind
love is…

9-1-1

It is finally spring, or hope eternal.
They had a church stop today,
and barber shop too. And ordinary
sidewalk by the lovely green park.
And now, after a earned respite
of half-eaten baloney sandwiches
trees whirl another chorus line.
Hyacinths aside the bank encourage
investment, as life is for investing.
Daffodils of the embankment smear.
Forsythia betwixt the two ways
appear swift as the soon to be summer.
Even now as it is the cold of winter,
and life has its bite, so goes hope.
Their feet have awaited this bloom
and they go steady upon the petals
as life moves, moves, 365, 24-7,
moves cardinals again to spring.

And so, their sirens do.

In Position to Heal

Out of the ice storm
into this concrete spiral of a parking garage
all the celestial bodies orbit and pass.
And she now takes her space as designated.
She knows her spot right here next to the Dodge.

She wonders how many may recognize her face
without the mask. And see her father.
In blasting heat of Scotland, Mississippi,
he had died face down in a pig farm.

She learned of lives eventually failing to breathe.
And she steps every day upon this rigor mortis.
Life never seems long enough lukewarm.

And he, well, he was greatest man she ever knew.
She walks swiftly.
A body in motion tends to remain.
He'd want it that way. Her patients are in place.

Hippocratic Oath

In the armamentarium,
so much to know.
And so much to never forget.
Let truth appear out in the open
in its depth, in its stair
through the open chest.

Goes the promise
clear as first sight of blood,
even when so much has passed.
Life, stubborn and fragile,
knows death.
Fate knows a professional title,
and in the end could care less.

The world turns its pained face.
So much to know.

The voice of the oath knows life
is to live and to live it blessed.
A self to give.

So much to know.
World turns its pained face.
And we remember.

Emergency Room Floor

I see it.
It seems real.
Fake grain simulating hard wood.

If only I'd feel the same
of the bits and pieces of me
that land upon it blood red.

How far splatters a broken heart?
It makes its shapes,
each a face I love and know so well.

Deep within me
I rather feel no floor.
Rather let go to fly.

But, for now, beyond time,
I give in, and give all of me,
ever real, to the grain.

Behind the Wheel

Astounding it is
how we are made to heal.
No dying truck can do such.
Call me trite, but
my right ventricle bleeds
not motor oil, but
that hope to heal.

This auto mechanic, me,
wants to be home with you.
Home so we can schmooze
our hours of pure nonsense,
such as color of window treatments,
dishes, wishes, dishwasher,
all pure love.

Love, love, love,
a word seemingly
thrown around so much.
All this as
stripes on the asphalt pierce
like spears of screwdrivers.

And as I right-to-left shunt
right atrium home,
the right ventricle is never alone,
but with you.
All this is in mind as

this heart is wrenched
and under attack.

Hold me. Wherever you now are.
You know me. Tell me,
we'll get it all fixed
and good as new.
All I can think of
in this breaking heart of mine
is you.

Poor Historian

Time flies.

If only I had been a fly on this guy's previous wall, then I'd know it all. His ailments, his anguished bones. I could then give the blind side due hell. His demons might fall with justified smart bombing. And yet, what of any collateral damage? What of children still stuck in his head?

I know I know so much. I know I care, and maybe that's most important. It's why for now at this very moment, I know I have the world to learn. I start with the vitals.

Our Arrival at General

We've been up before the sun
and stand here now aside the forsythia
spotlighted by ray of lamppost
here outside this hospital, long
this stone fortress we'd rather run from.

Two birds observe us from their tightrope.
And we pause, long enough awake
to discover the tone of light at horizon.
So much ahead, so much already here,
and we see each other, the shared fear.

And we hear birdsong our hope onward.
Nothing weird to our ears, the birds.
You see the rising orange hue as I do.
With a knowing smile and long breath,
we walk through the glass doors.

Welcome

Don't bandage the sun.
Let it hemorrhage.
So much of it is a gift that gives.
Best when shared with everyone.
Do you feel the warmth?

I see the light above me
even though eyes are sealed.
It reveals through the lids and
follows me through the corridors.
Please don't forget my face,
my aging windows, brick façade.

Open door dissipates the shadows.
Visitors must wear their own face.
Home is for the remembering,
for the nourishing, for the entering.
For the greeting of light inside.

Even if so hard to see under blinds,
so bound and mummified in sheets,
please take a seat.

And share the warmth, the light.

Patience Is a Virtue

And in our need for the virtue
we take a number.

And in our need for the virtue
we fall in line.

And in our need for the virtue
we wait to arrive.

If only we would realize,
we are already here

with the virtue patiently waiting.

Patience Is Power

It runs like a racehorse.
And I am only able to uncontrollably tap my feet.

My prayer is for grace for the pace of being stuck.
But I have so little trace waiting for Dr. Longwait.

Popular Mechanics is here, and a muscled Mustang.
Silly me, just open up the silly magazine.

What a beautiful red machine, standing still, so fast.
I remember that year, the pain, yet surviving 2008.

I can go on and on about it, but why now complain.
Rather read this as fast as I can before being called in.

Yes, amazing how quick the prayers are answered
for grace.

Waiting Room

We each speak like an iguana.

Unless, it's actually
we've finally fallen fast asleep.

Then we each sleep like an iguana
until a name sounds household.

Telescope

Just a Surprise Lily, that's probably what it is. Or perhaps some kind of hybrid. Or maybe just another scientifically named diagnosis for just another form of the varied amaryllis up on a hill on a faraway field, now not so very far at all. Doc would know, judging by the diploma on the wall. Like a firefighter at blistering door, she would sense what she's in for.

"Say ahhhh," she says with depressor. But what does she see?

We can imagine.

Maybe deep, dark caves, red flames, tongue of fire humongous, a dragon. Or just a frog. Maybe only last week's once tasty soufflé. Or a spare tire, a red wagon, a choir of birds, or lots of fog.

Maybe, even lost words, slippery as germs, those hard to say terms, ones we thought we might say, or thought we did, but apparently got lost on the way, now all moldy and hairy.

Or maybe pronouncements so very classy, dressed in robes in a place sacred as a chapel, no reason to be scared, with a staircase up a bell tower, with rope from Adam's apple to swing back and forth the Hunchback of Notre Dame pleading sanctuary.

So much to diagnose under a nose.

But, likely just another amaryllis growing up on a hill. And she would know.

needle

like a sudden storm

goes
carries
takes
throws
all that's left

we may suppose

may suppose
we too shall finally leave
and then
the end

but maybe
we may come to believe
we remain
all along
much more than this gust
of wind

maybe peace awaits
underneath
like a sudden awakening

for the bereft

as if yes

like rain

brings forth the flowers

Running Tests

These and those, you're busy,
I hope, while I sit and wait.
What contorts claustrophobic,
maybe this you can heal, this soul.

Now that there's this brain scan,
see what more you may find.

See what may be top of mind.
And go deep underneath.

You might even see all the cosmos.
Maybe even yourself.

My Chest X-ray

What constellation,
what stardust fireworks,
what dying star, black hole,
what light travels
deep to my soul?

Come see and be lost in me.

Find space where we may share
a breath

of universe.

Beyond this Cancer

You love me.

All of me.
Despite the parts that are not me.

Erase
all that was and find what is
always ready to be made.

Soon,
so much drifts away.

Not us.

We shall stay.

Love is built that way.

Our Living Room

Our living room is far down the hall, past the janitor's hideout in this place. It's down the hall. Somewhere far down the hall. My eyes go there. Maybe all my hopes and dreams. Maybe just skin remains here in the gloom of this present room.

But I am not going to dream of somewhere far away. I am here. So, I must make myself to be. Here. With you.

And what to make of lovely you? I love when you reappear.

I have always loved how our home positions itself under the wide, wonderful sky. And how June has a way of sun. Splashed upon us and everyone. And how June stays, even to winter's darkest days. Through you.

In my current disarray, how much of the cosmos are in my eyes? And in yours? How far apart are the stars? Are we yet still close, body and out of body, now as you hold my nearly incapable hand? Help me to understand. What lingers near as new?

More than any dissipating dream, there is you. Stay here with me in what was once, and forever will be, our living room.

Hope Is My Critical Condition

Robust green the oak
outside this window.
Hope is the last leaf
on what might seem to others
a totally barren tree,
but simply is as it is, green.

Spread wide the blinds
and let me see all of Hope.
Indeed for a moment
I wonder if it can be a gift,
this discomfort, this here
and now which leaves past
my earlier normalcy.
For now is rescued by Hope.

Not a wishful thinking,
but an expectancy of now,
as now keeps arriving. Enfolds,
it does, once a little cocoon
wrapped ever so tightly, lovingly,
to this, my present condition,
to envision the butterfly nearby
fluttering normally.

I need these wings.
Don't be so surprised if you see
these majesties full of life,
my eyelids boisterously.

For I am, even for a moment alight,
living my now
in whatever diagnosis this is,
as the gifted present flight of me.
And I am circling this tree of life,
this me as I am.

No Long Face

And he sees his mother at the door.
Her precious, loving smile.

She too is Hope.

Give me that very balm, he prays.

What does he look like to her?
How does he now appear
to his long lost deceased mother?

Let it indeed be Hope.

Like her.

Hope Is More than a Placebo

Hope
has a way of texture,
has a way of deep import

as forever,
unfathomable and
yet simple as if to a child,

like a hand
firm as a father's,
even long after he's gone.

Waiting on a Miracle

Will wine ever flow despite all the vinegar in my veins?

I know it shall arrive, the balm, whatever its welcoming face, sure as all anointing oils, sure as all the saints who return to my door.

I am blessed that this old, bold hope endures. With hope, even now is joy.

So it is I sense the imminent cure, and I shall wait this way, even now, this stay as splendor, yes even now, here near as all heaven rises from a trace of swirling lavender somewhere within this skin of alabaster.

Pain

You ask for a number,
1 to 10.

I fear
beyond this tearing of me,

I fear I may receive what I now want,
and embrace it as my own,

the numbers going numb.

Right Now, It Hurts

On a scale of one to ten,
I defer to the next breath.
Pardon me if I put off rigor mortis
in my smile for the time being.

Rather it be a freewheeling version,
a smile that would cast no aspersion,
but be respectful for what is genuine,
for we are all a bit long faced of late.

O, I will not hide it when it formulates,
and so feel free to react your own way.
Let it be real, and it does not have to stay,
for life has its emotions that roll away,
and night does take its turn with day.

Granted, this ailment has a demanding,
hard to rhyme name, but shortens
with you and me together simply here.

Help me to endure this pain.

All along,
let our vision be a countenance true
through all the varied numbers.
For we will have given it all
to higher stuff where miracles begin,
no matter the measure far beyond ten.

Simply,
thank you for being with me as I am.

The Lady with the Lamp

In her hands, this angelic being carries the sun.
She is replicated in all angelic beings, but perhaps
she is the only one.

Here I am in exhaustion, my weakness, and she
touches my forehead. So much sky in my dreams,
yet lack of eye to see. She hears me.

Allows me to lift my soul above this indented bed.
Allows me the sky to run.
I have read what Longfellow has written of her,

passing through the glimmering glow. She knows
all my numbers, my data, simplified. She is so wise
in what she does here amidst the wounded and weary.

She says when she is no longer a memory,
just a name somehow said, may her voice perpetuate.
And yes, she tends to me again and again.

And yes, she is in all these angelic beings,
as if the only one.
And yes, Florence Nightingale has a way of rising

like each new sun.

Stubborn

Despite stretched hours,
blurred clock face,
and despite wires, hoses, beeping,
that beeping, beeping
ventilator, and despite long facades
of doctors, parades
of very likable nurses and pillows
and pills,
        we know time to be short.

Back home
baby brother Charlie tells us by phone
it's starting to snow.

And we know that despite cold walkway,
spring's still lifting them up—
dad's long ago planted daffodils.

And maybe that's why the old man here
is obstinately pointing at door.

Wants us to get the beep out of here,
walk pass those daffodils and be there.

After all, he says,
what in the beep are we leaving Charlie
home all alone for?

Pill

Doctor,
what have you wrapped into this seed?
How many hours, dollars, are packed
industriously into this space, this ability
of ours to be just in time to sit and to survive
jail and railroads.

Hurry, Doctor,
my grandchildren are waiting for me to play.
I guess it's a roll of the dice, but a toss I'll take.

Mother would always say,
each comes with a dose of poison, these pills
for all the world's ills.
The side effects will likely give me whiskers
and stripes and then also sharpen my fangs.

O, to some maybe it's just a cardboard box
sealed here compact and not meant to be opened.
But for some, like us, life is made to be played.
There's treasured endurance to this Monopoly.
My grandkids will visit me at Park Place.

Under the tongue, you say, and let it be opened.

And look! So many places to rent or to buy.
None of it with more curb appeal than time,
lined with a pathway of boisterous tiger lilies.

Sighting Bedside

The winter is so cold, it burns. Even under sheets.
I touch the summer beach at the corner of my eyes.
I have a friend on TV. We share Swiss cheese.
But, so many new things I seem to quickly forget.
Like where I am, what I can be, and simply who.

But at least the old stuff stays old, and not too new.
Stays around like air, which is what I always need.
Even if rather stale. Great things are in store for me.
I trust the air in the tires stay stable where I parked.
I often ask for ginger ale, because it is so bubbly.

So, I'm in for a transplant of some sort, so they say,
and so they had fully explained, and so I had signed
so many lines along the way, and it's going to cost
an arm and a leg. But there at the end of the bed,
there they are, Cosmas and Damian, doctors, saints.
Yes, I'll be in good shape. Especially, after settling
the future billing complaints. There are things to see.

And hear. I really like the sound of the word—
Fluorescent. Is it emission of light, or of flowers?
Or both? Or is it efflorescence? Or is that more of a
powdery residue down my arms like on fresh loaves
of warm bread. Or is it effervescent, like bubbly?
Like full of life. Like trust in good Jesus, yes,
that all will be alright. Like ginger ale just arrived.

Competence

And now, here is this doctor. She is a good one. Not just because there are so many valid frames on her wall. She listens. And, she tells me like it is. She comes from the other side of the world, but her presence is right here. Her eyes are wise, with compassion. Acknowledges that I exist.

I ask her how much she actually knows. She seems humble about it, but I get to hoping that it's much. A good doctor, like any pro, is hard to know.

I have some experience in seeking appropriate know-how. Last summer, we thought it would be just a tune-up. Turned out to be engine Armageddon. Our auto mechanic did everything he could. Made his cuts and hammered. Then wiped his hands and dropped the hood. Then asked what our house needed. Handyman Jack of all Trades finally admitted that while he probably could fix shoes, not so much brake shoes. His know-how was just better with wood.

And the other expert we prized, he had Einstein hair. We knew he was smart and fearless for the mission. Our electrician. After the fire, he went on to other missions.

As for this physician, she elaborates on the litany of what is ahead, every step, and then smiles with a gentle but firm way of confidence. I smile too. After all, when it comes down to it, healing is contagious. Despite all that feels lousy, this somehow feels good.

My Life Is in Your Hands

They say

faith can move a mountain.

Now,
I've placed my trust.

Please move this small lump.

Spring Fever

Doctor,
I'll ask this with patient etiquette.

Ease that vane
as it wickedly twists.

But give life to the flag
by enabling the spirit to flow.

Allow the frozen snow, once so silent,
to sing down my spouts
like winter has broken.

Simply said,
I rather that we make it so very easy.

I'll take two daffodils
and call you in the morning.

Wet Puma in the Vestibule

I'm waiting for this latest fever to break.
It has caught me to the old age bones
just to rattle my ribs like swaying chimes.

Now the wind brings in the mountains
of dark clouds tight to my neck. Brings
the electrifying wide sky to a grumble

and the loose teethe to seethe. And then
I have one of them there dreams of me
moseying aimlessly through my familiar,

now suddenly unfamiliar shadowy town
in my dry and ever vintage blue Clydes,
those great old sneakers I wish I still had.

But I'm stressed to remember the way,
realizing, man, things are just so distant,
so discombobulating walking in the rain.

Again, then, I see my mother at the door.
She's reminding me not to mess the floor.
So, I'm here, back home finally, yes, yes!

Need now my long gone sneaks to breathe.
Hate for these to be all soppy and heavy.
Yet, to be honest, they still look at ease.

Being home.

Aspirate

So much gets in the way.
So much is not me,
yet so close to me, like every breath
as if part of me, but ephemeral
like the leaves of our family tree.

So much is meant to leave.
So much more, to stay.

I shall
open my mouth and fight for air.
I shall speak,
but my words may drift incoherent.
So much dissipates.
And the family tree bends.

The nurses, doctors, poke.
They poke somewhere deep into me.

I mumble a Hail Mary.

And soon,
even though all shall pass,
and even as
all the atmosphere shall break,
shall flatten to faint doldrums,

I breathe.

Appendix

Don't let it be the heart, this part to go vestigial, as if all that evolves connects us less to heaven. Need the heart to beat, so to love and move the feet. Things have their function and then again who knows. Some roads drift to sea, if only for the lovely view. And such purpose may never be even used.

Some things spread out as if only supplementary, an accessory part of sorts, not even a necessity. We have a lawn out back.

This thing needing to come out of me, I have no clue of its use, not quite a donut spare in the trunk. No full-sized Goodyear, for sure, with usable tread.

They say your back bone is connected to your shoulder bone. Your shoulder bone is connected to your neck bone. Some things stray away, but everything is connected in some way.

We have a shed out back but we pay a guy to mow the lawn. So, no mower storage needed. But instead we do store in there nice and neat the hammock, too rarely connected tree to tree, if at all ever strung and used.

And so, the appendix had just burst. It was there, near the junction, or so I gather by trust, where small intestine meets large. I don't know its original function but it has got me talking now to a nurse who happens by fate to be mother of the guy who mows. And when I get home, I'm for sure laying in that hammock over the fresh green. Unless the hammock is a mess. Then we'll disconnect that for the trash, and I'll just lay on the grass.

Bilocate

I'm bedridden and stuck,
but
the outside ice cream truck
is a summer melody
so cool,
somewhat.

Dusk likes to dance.
We sit at end of the rocks,
our feet wading a wake.
Sun runs to a ripple.

When here,
and when away,
I glide by faith.
Let me leave.
Let me arrive
not a moment too late.

I have a cup of ice cream.

Such a kind nurse.
She's also given to me the sky
blue socks.

even as I sleep

this malady, I guess, was meant to be.
I further guess what is next is up to me,
not to give in, and I won't.
but to let go.
see, I am blessed not to suffer this alone.
there is an army all around me.

my body is universal flesh and bone
destined to earth, like stone, finite.
yet, heaven is here, I cannot deny.
see how healing love runs through me.
I too am made of love beyond breath.
I see angels all around my bed.

Open My Blind

Raise my bed,
turn my head,
shut Wheel of Fortune
and let me look out glass
instead.

Somewhere
there's a pretty city.

I wish it may mirror me.

Maybe, just maybe,
I can reflect.

May it not be the back
of a stinking smoke stack
unless
I truly look like dreck.

And if I'm that way dreck
then call the doctor back.

The me I want to be
is the pretty city.

Not Yet Left the Building

Elvis,
with a twist of the radio dial,
stands up quick
as a Casey Kasem hit
and with white sheet
still caped upon him
allows his legs to freely twitch.

And in our beds we are inspired,
for here right now
at this very nursing home
he too is free as he always was
and always will be, to be the king.

For, he's just heard for the first time
yet again
It's Now or Never.

We all should be so busy, living.

One World in Hospice

In many ways, all of us are here,
all of life is this, the wishing for a cure,
the desire for peace.

So much hurt in this world.
So much hurt in ourselves.
So much to ease.

Where to start?

Unfortunately,
all around us we neglect to see.
The good Lord is within all our faces.

I think of that now
and how a shared smile
                    can begin with me.

And see how vibrant this earth can be.

Give

We all should care. For each other. That is what Simon the janitor just said. Moment ago, I tried a drive toward the rim in this very old basketball gym, but am now flat in the lane, apparently dead. Maybe I am losing my leather with so much to remember, but I hear this is widely going around. Lack of blood pressure, air pressure, air.

Now, this janitor, this Simon, or an angel instead does CPR.

And soon doctors will operate on my arteries. Open heart surgery, to my appreciation, will be the repair.

As for Simon in this gym, maybe no one before had ever seen him. May never again. But, then again, hopefully they will. After all, we all should care, Simon says.

Open Heart

Awe is open. Part the sea, let them see love as bled, and familiarize the huddle around the patient, by him unseen, but the sharing of utensils shiny and clean. Threaded knives visit veins where life is led. Blood flows. Open chestnut does what it could. Beat, it does, alive. Open heart, open wide.

Put them all aside. Make room for two, for husband and wife on this hot afternoon. From the porch upon which he now steps forward, all of Eden to see, and hear, he is home. Yes, piano plays as only she could, somewhere beyond the door in the living room where the living should.

He knows his wife had died like this. And now upon his bed, with all his insides shed of disguise, he opens his heart again for her, and she for him. They meet on that porch swing, smiling over glasses of lemonade. Time doesn't pass, for anesthesia never does. And time somewhere just stays as it is. Plains must await earth's wheat, but forever is what it is.

Reins are pulled complete. Pins tie back the folds, but hold to engine. Skins again shield this one, twined by surgeon. Arteries, mysteries, so much more to know till death depart. And soon, reigns come and go as this bed now rolls like all trains.

Notify the family of the good news in the waiting room of prayer. Wait till they hear that PopPop saw MomMom through heaven's shade to share her piano played. And then her precious lemonade!

Beauty Tip

With love and faith
as a foundation base,
put on grace.

I know this as she smiles
and pulls off my mask,
all my bullheaded bandages.

She softly says
it's so good to see me
as I am.

And I see her eyes
as flowers bloom
all over the place.

Ho' oponopono

We sit and try to talk.
Paradise is down the hall,
far beyond the exit door.
Pineapple had traveled
all the way, all the way here.
I'd rather travel to it.
          Hawaii.
  Rather outside sit.
See the sea, and feel
   the mist.

But then again,
everything's so close.
    I can feel it.
Close as Kansas City to here.
  Close as Kansas
        to Missouri.
So much missed
  being so far from you.
And we share it from a dish.

And the illness of my heart
   hurts all of me
but we smile somehow
  over the pineapple.
I forget the reasons
  I tried to stop loving you.
Because I've never stopped.

Maybe forgiveness is my start
healing all of me.
And divided islands cluster
sliver by segment,
by carved wedge,
piece by peace.

Cord

Long ago we had our bond. Still do,
but with less blood flow. I'll always be
your mother, even though sometimes
I forget. After all, see, I lost my eyes
somewhere.

Much can be said about sight.
I do recognize you by your presence.

We both somehow breathe
and have given each other life.

You're just beautiful. Now go. Just go.
Go home and kiss those beautiful kids
for me goodnight.

Within these Wounds

Like the Angels in my hospital room, I play ball.
So much runs timeless within, even in delays,
ages upon ages upon me, and I am now here
contemplating the other cross nailed to the wall,
one hanging there silently next to my game and
it knows me, somehow as if high fiving me.

Because of it, maybe I am more than my box,
more than what confines me here, stuck in time
thinking Angels and passage of boyhood time
while the clock, which holds nothing, gestures
superficially at the bottom of the 9th on the wall.
Like the Angels in this place, I am clockless.

Nursing Home Piano

I shall pass it again, and remember the high school stage, all the foreground blackness as if I could sense all of outer space ahead beyond all our instruments. And somehow back then it seemed as if it all would be played somewhere in my head. But now, soon it shall be lunch, and down this ephemeral hall the spokes on the wheels shall barely blur on by. And by some grace maybe we may come to believe we remain all along much more than this present gust of wind.

Somewhere within the clouded grain, and underneath the yellow smile, maybe fake, or not, somewhere within the skin, within the box somewhat also too hidden, maybe forgotten, somewhere within the timber, the timbre awaits. Somewhere all of life's splendor is far more than antique furniture or tree or paneling or wood or tired peeling name, or all that once was, or only the breeze, but remains. Somewhere outside in the cold, the brittle brown leaves hold tight to the pin oak, even in the icy rain.

Wet Windows

There is a melting statue outside of who,
I don't know. Seems sad if we are numb
to who a memorial memorializes. Maybe
it's just a generic metal angel. Fake,

unlike what is inside here. Unlike
the soaked umbrella you now shake.
Good to know, we are made to heal. And
here we go, just in time to watch TV.

The Weather Channel. You say this place
is a peaceful place and that my face is grace.
I say, yours is so good to see. Both of us
share the rarity of a horseshoe cloud and

the suddenly rediscovered radar of eternity.
My guess is we'd rather first handedly talk
about the weather, even if it's just so far
outside our walls, by the statue, and pouring

forever out there. But in here, well, here
that freedom to endlessly rain feels just right.
So, my son, let us share our dreams inside,
the wide sky of heaven within our wet eyes.

Certain

I will die.
Eventually.
That closing occurrence,
that happening in time
will arrive.

But, until then,
beyond the grip of time,
there is this
anointed moment.

Followed by this.

And the next.

Love provides breath
by timeless breadth.

And all around me,
the selfless fully know
all the joy
of being alive endless,
knowing that forever
is the stuff
for every moment.

This moment.

Followed by this.

playing tag

gotch u next time
should you fall
like heaven
like a leaf
like an acorn
like peace of a kite
long lost twisted
up a pine
or a ball in a gutter
gotch you next time
into my hands
cupped and ready
just as you have done
you stranger angel

in saving my life.

Heal

The injury to that broken mop
didn't heal itself.
Healing takes tending in the mending.
This you know and
you've returned now with it good as new.
And here you are with a smile for me
while humming *Amazing Grace*
with this bandaged mop skillfully swirling.

In this immobile, highway of a place,
in this space consecrated by weakness,
even as the others are now off stage,
here you are, with strength
all about healing.
Here you are shining the floor
from all my disgust as you ably whirr
miracles brought forth to a sheen.

Me, I have asked the cosmos why,
just why am I here?
And you say in your own clear way:
for the glory of God.
Here we all are as we are,
gifted and sacrificing despite any stain,
and smiling, believing, allowing
miracles to be, as God wills of us
nothing short of love.

Life is a shared parade of angels
as together with the good Lord we go
walking across any impossible sea.
And the world with all its nagging,
all its bruises and pain, feels the healing
powered by grace.

And here you are with your kind face.
Here we all are, somehow face to face.
To be healing.

www.ingramcontent.com/pod-product-compliance
Lightning Source LLC
Chambersburg PA
CBHW022159160726
48282CB00024B/258
* 9 7 8 9 3 9 5 2 2 4 1 1 6 *